South Gosforth 1st School

GW01417563

Contents

Why is blood so important?

Your body is full of organs, and all your organs are made up of cells. The cells work very hard to keep you alive, but they need feeding, with a gas called **oxygen** and with food to give them **energy**. The blood looks after all those cells, because it gives them the oxygen and food they need, and takes away other gases and waste that the body can do without.

This book tells you how it all works!

Blood travels all around the body

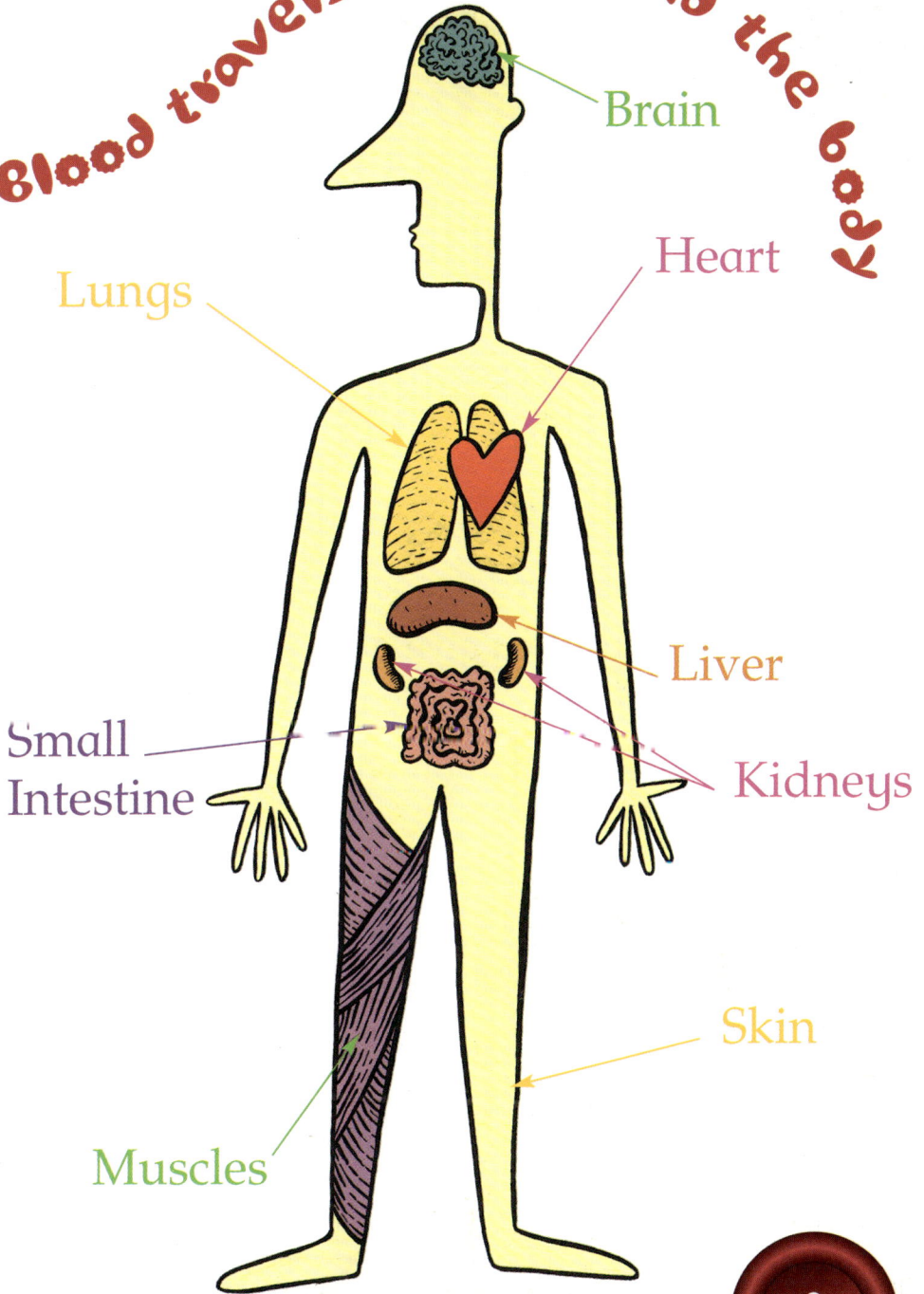

Brain

Heart

Lungs

Liver

Small
Intestine

Kidneys

Muscles

Skin

What is blood made of?

Blood looks red and watery. But if you look at it closely under a microscope you can see different sorts of blood cells. They all have their own job to do.

Red blood cells carry oxygen round the body. They give our blood its colour. There are 200 million of these cells in one tiny drop of blood.

Plasma makes up half your blood. It's what the other cells float in. It also carries the food, gases and wastes – the things that the body has to use or lose.

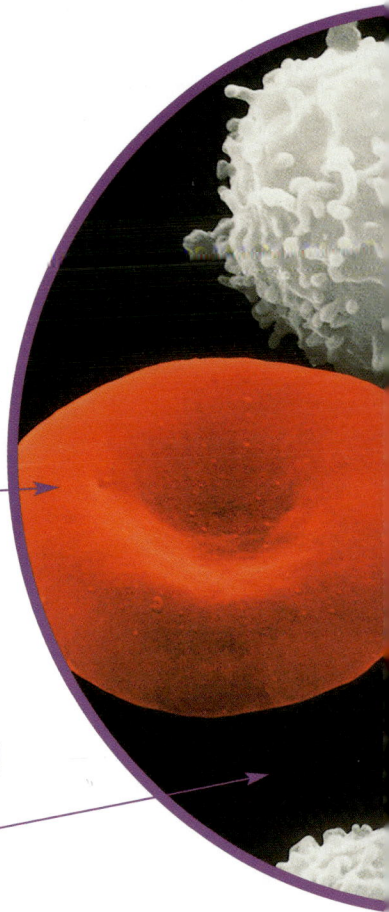

White blood cells defend our bodies from dangers like infections. Some of them attack and "eat up" up enemy germs.

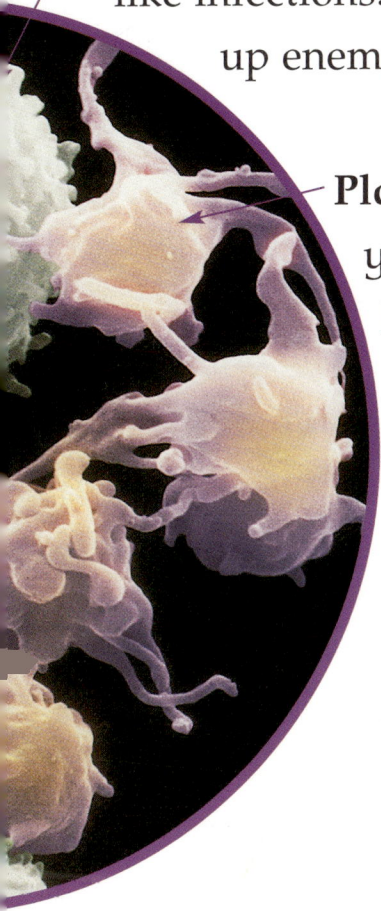

Platelets make blood clot when you cut yourself or graze your knee. They plug the hole in the skin. If they didn't, you would bleed and bleed.

This photograph was taken through a microscope.

FACTS

- Red and white blood cells are made in your bones.

- Blood is 79 per cent water.

- The body makes 140 million red blood cells a minute! That number is more than twice the population of Britain.

- Blood weighs 6–10 per cent of your total body weight!

How does blood travel round the body?

Your body has a great network of tubes, big and small, to carry your blood. These tubes are called blood vessels. The one-way system guides blood from the pumping heart to every cell in the body. This journey round the body is called **blood circulation**.

There are two main types of blood vessel–arteries and veins.

- The **arteries** carry blood away from the pumping heart. They need to be strong, and they have thick elastic walls.

- **Veins** carry blood back to the heart. Veins do not have to be as strong as arteries do, and they have thinner walls. They have **valves** – like little trapdoors – to make sure the blood flows only in one direction.

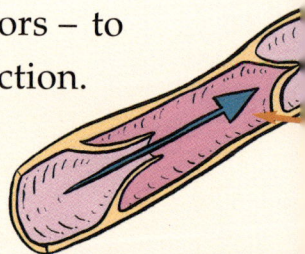

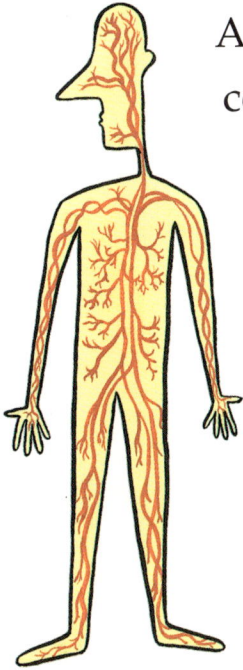

Arteries carry blood to every cell of your body, and to do this, each artery gets smaller and smaller, and narrower and narrower. To reach every cell, an artery must be as thin as a hair. When an artery is very thin, it is called a **capillary**.

a capillary, the blood cells have to travel in single file.

The food and oxygen then squeeze through the capillary walls into the cells of the body.

Blood can only go one way.

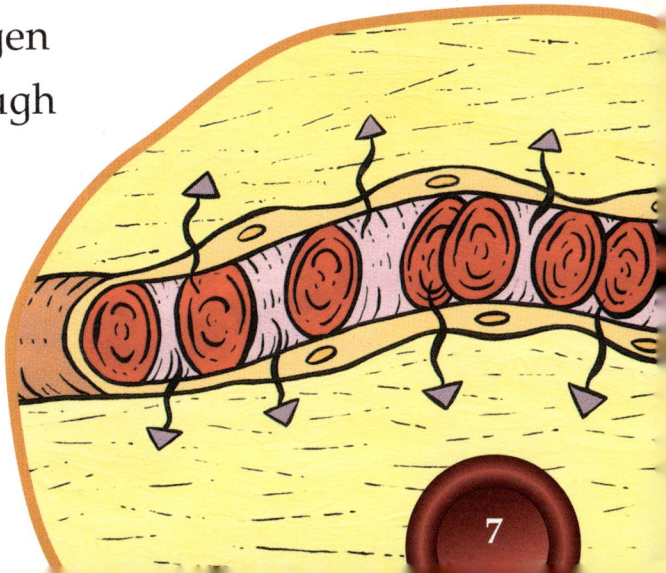

7

What happens to blood in the heart?

The heart is a strong pump that pumps the blood round the body. It pumps thousands of times a day, all through your life.

The heart is hollow, and inside there are four chambers. It is divided into two sides; and there are two chambers on each side. Blood goes through the heart twice – once on each side.

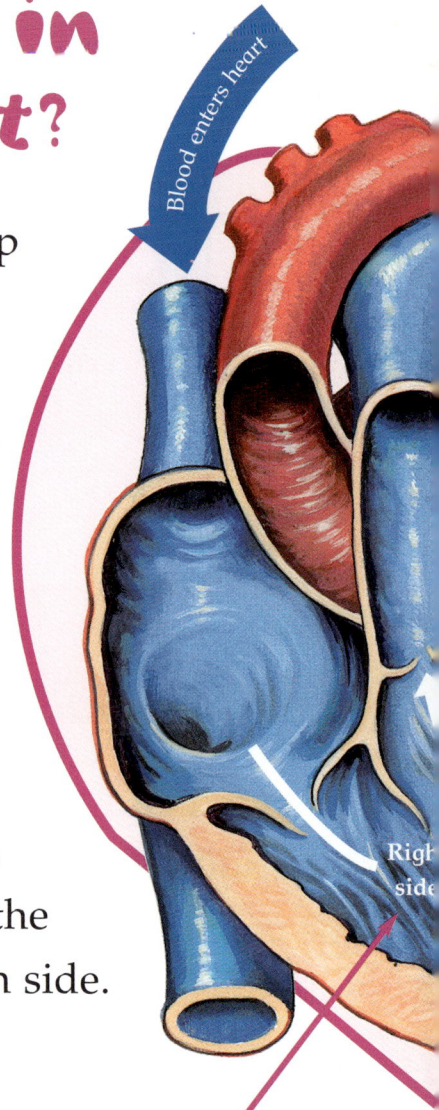

Blood enters heart

Right side

The right side of the heart pumps blood to the lungs.

Left side

The first time the blood is pumped to the lungs to pick up oxygen. Then the blood goes back to the heart to be pumped round the rest of the body, taking oxygen to all your cells.

The blood can flow in only one direction round the body – out from the heart, round the body and back to the heart. Like a one-way traffic system in a town, it passes all the important places on its route.

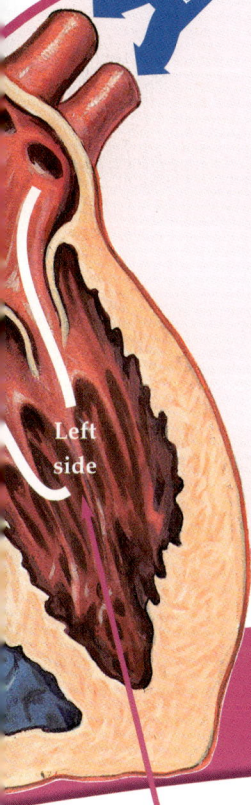

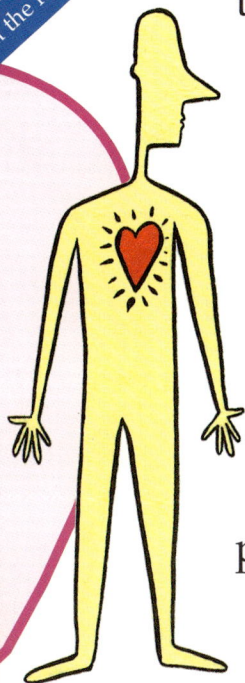

But this trip takes only ninety seconds!

The left side of the heart takes blood from the lungs and pumps it it out to the body.

9

What happens to blood in the lungs?

The lungs have to get as much oxygen into your blood as possible, and to get rid of another gas called **carbon dioxide** which the body doesn't want.

The lungs are full of tiny balloons called **alveoli** which are surrounded by tiny capillaries.

FACT

- There are 300 million tiny airbags or alveoli in each lung.

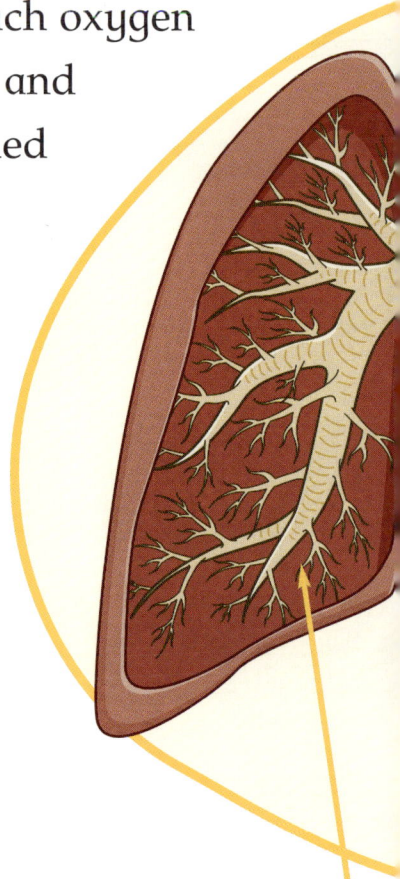

You breathe in through your windpipe and the air goes down into branching tubes called bronchioles. These bronchioles end in tiny air sacs called alveoli.

Windpipe

When you breathe in, air fills these balloons, and the oxygen squeezes out of the alveoli and into the tiny blood vessels. The oxygen is then taken round the body to all the body's cells. At the same time, carbon dioxide that the body doesn't want passes from the blood in the capillaries into the alveoli, ready to be breathed out.

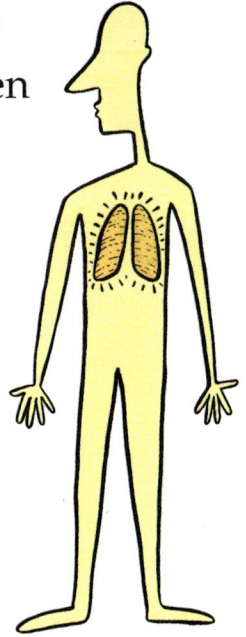

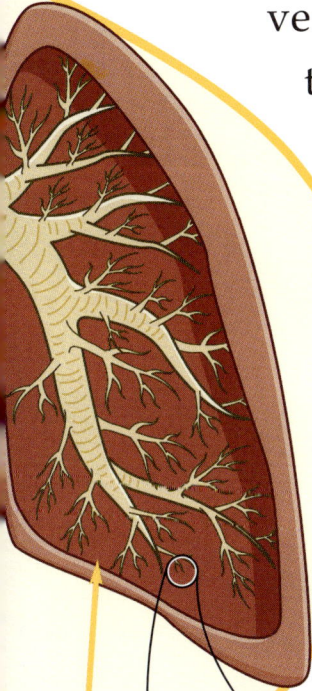

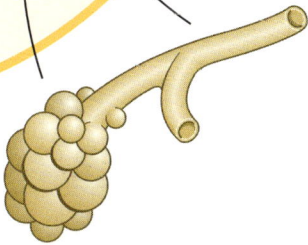

Breathing in

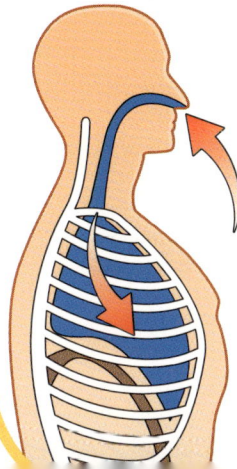

Breathing out

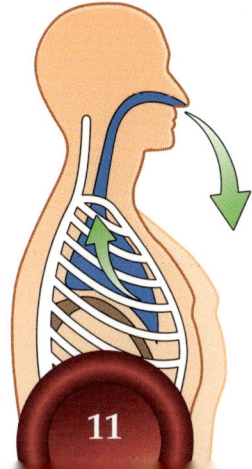

Each alveolus is covered with little capillaries

11

What happens to blood in the brain?

Your brain controls everything you do.

So if blood cannot reach your brain, even for ten seconds, you will lose **consciousness**. After a few minutes, you will die.

movement

behaviour and feelings

FACT

- The brain needs 35 litres of blood an hour so that its cells get the oxygen they need.

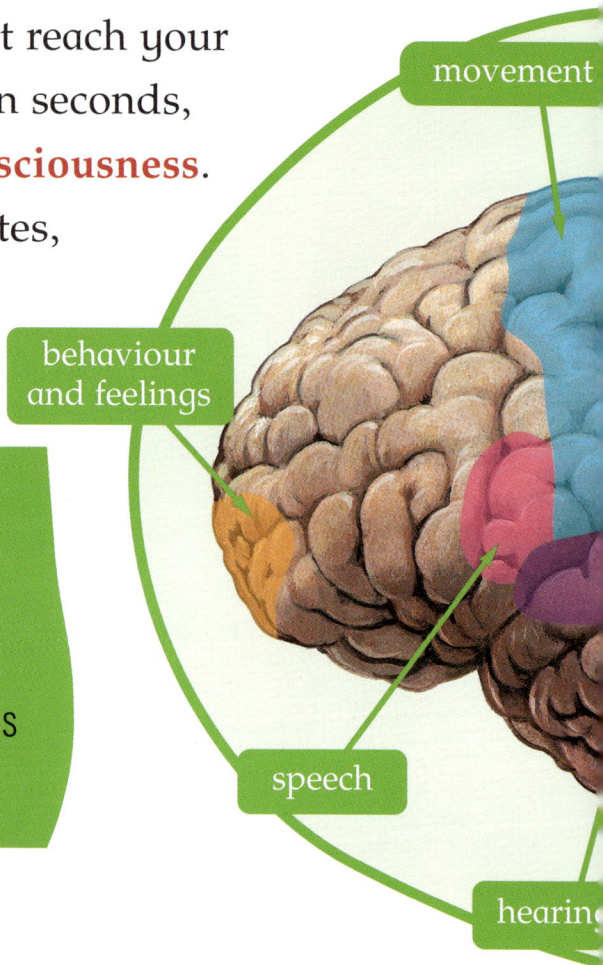

speech

hearing

Brain cells need lots of oxygen.
The heart pumps blood up through
the **carotid artery**, one of the biggest
arteries in the body. The brain is full of
cells just like the rest of the body.
When the blood reaches it, oxygen and
food enter the cells through the
capillaries, and the waste gases
leave in the same way. The
food is what gives your
brain energy to think!

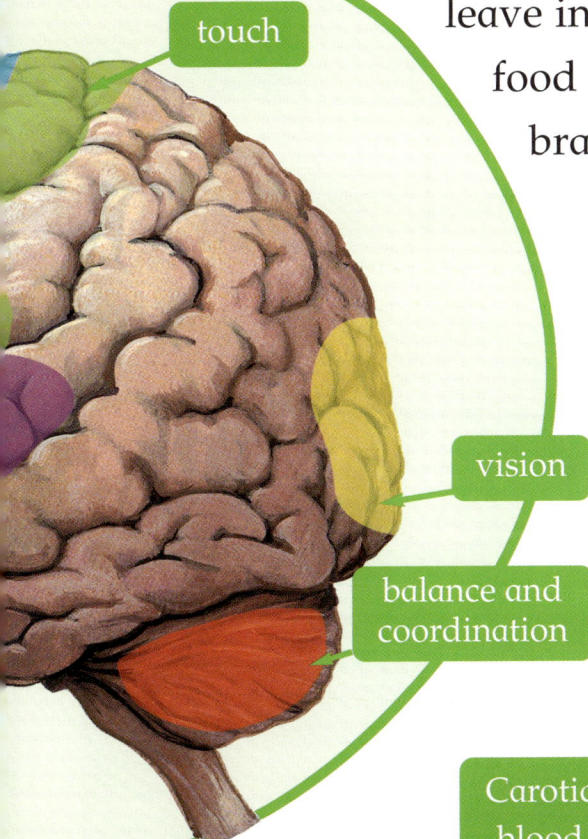

touch

vision

balance and
coordination

Carotid artery takes
blood to the brain.

What does blood do in the (small) intestine?

Your intestines are where the food you eat is broken down so that it can be used to keep the body alive. They are surrounded by those tiny blood vessels called capillaries. When you swallow your food, it goes down into your intestines, where it is broken down into **molecules**.

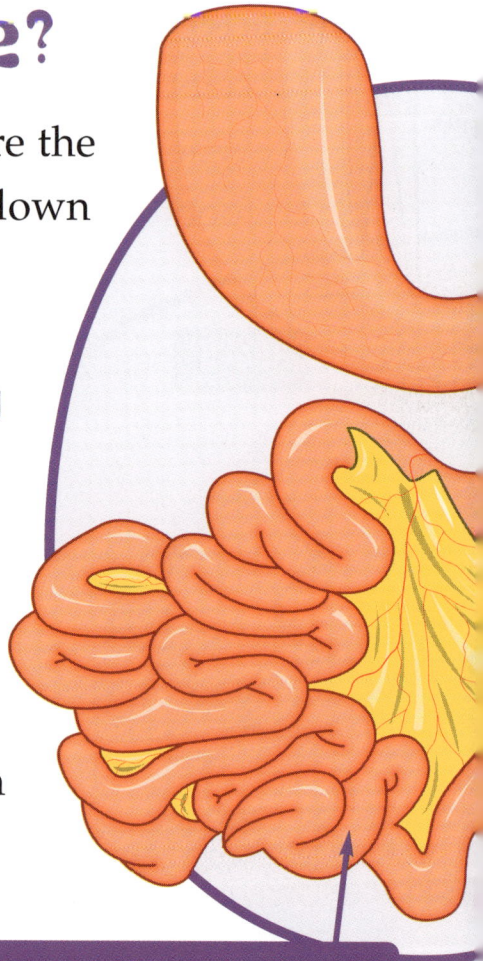

The intestines are folded up. This means that lots of capillaries can get very close to the walls of the intestine so as many food molecules as possible can pass into the blood.

The molecules are so small that they can pass through the intestine walls and then enter the blood-filled capillaries that are wrapped around the intestines.

- Different foods become different sorts of molecule.

- Meat and cheese become **protein** molecules, which help the body to grow and heal cells that get damaged.

- Potatoes and sugar become **glucose** molecules, which give the body energy.

- Fats and oils also give the body energy, but they are used to make cell walls too.

When you eat an orange, this is where the vitamin C from it reaches the bloodstream!

Cross-section of the small intestine. Molecules pass through these walls and into the bloodstream.

What happens to blood in the liver?

The blood carries the food molecules from the intestines to the liver. The liver decides what to do with them.

Imagine you have eaten a plate of fatty chips. The chips have been turned into fat molecules and glucose molecules in the intestines, so this is how they are when they reach the liver. Glucose is the body's number one fuel.

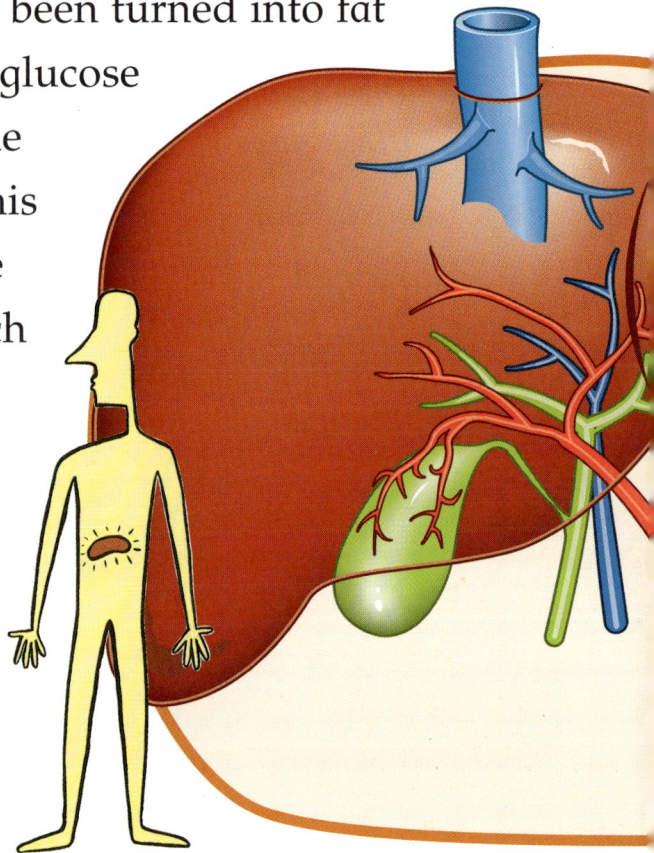

Your liver has to decide whether to store or use the glucose. The liver decides what your body needs. If the food is to be used right away, the blood cells carry it off round the body again.

Maybe your legs can use the glucose straight away!

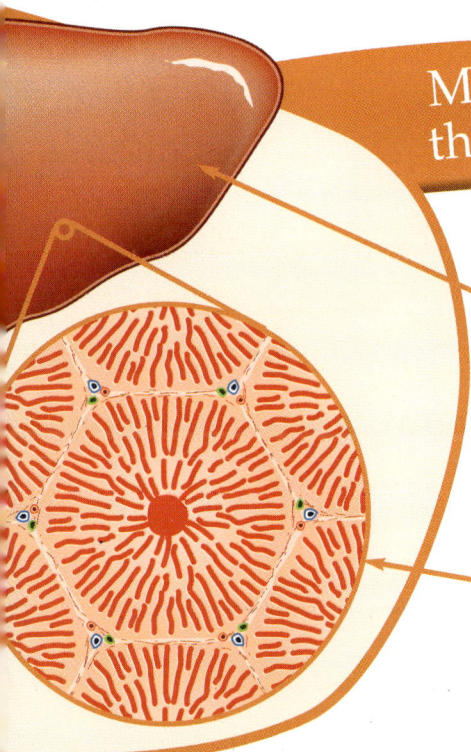

The liver is a simple organ made from thousands of hexagonal "boxes" called lobules.

Each lobule is encircled by capillaries. They bring food and take waste products away.

17

What happens to blood in the kidneys?

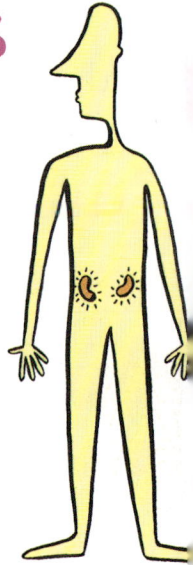

Every ten minutes all your blood goes through your kidneys.

The kidneys are like sieves that clean the blood by removing waste products.

This is how it works.

Your blood flows into the kidneys through tiny capillaries.

Glucose, salt and minerals are good for the body, so the kidneys make sure that these things go back into the bloodstream.

Things that are bad for your body, like poisonous wastes from the liver and the muscles, get mixed with water and pass out of the kidneys and into your bladder.

This is a cross-section of a kidney.

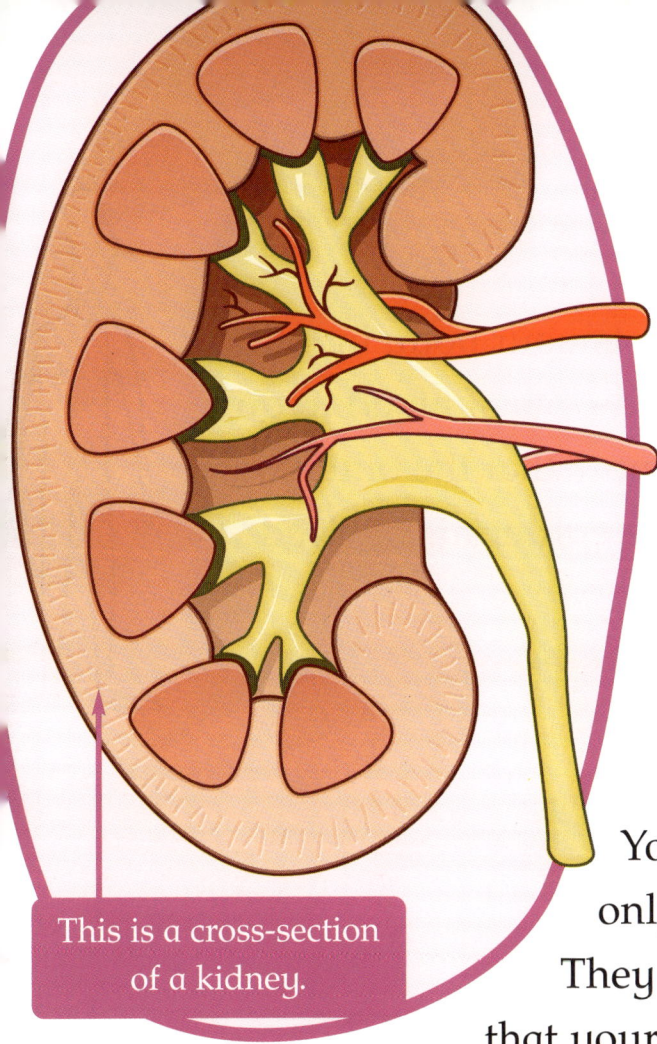

These poisons leave the body when you go to the toilet. If you have drunk a lot, your bladder fills up quickly, and you need to go to the toilet a lot.

Your kidneys not only clean your blood. They also make sure that your body has the right amount of water in it to keep it healthy. If your blood has too much water in it, the kidneys will take it away and send it to the bladder. If your body is short of water, the kidneys will leave what water there is in the blood.

What does blood do in the skin?

Your skin protects your body in lots of ways and it needs lots of blood to do this. Did you know that the outer layer of your skin, the **epidermis**, is dead?

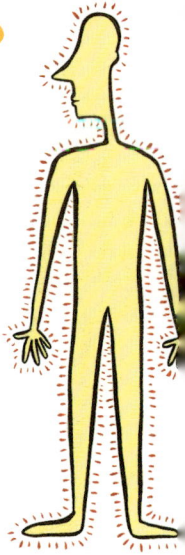

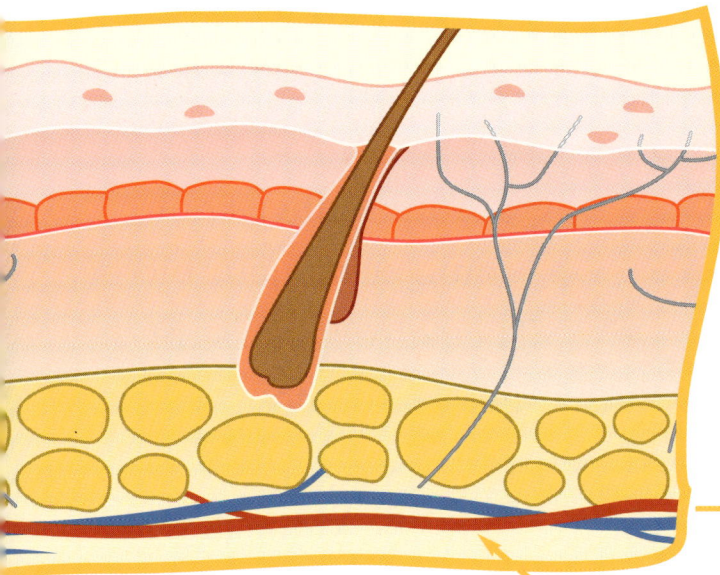

Cross-section of epidermis and dermis.

The epidermis is the protective out layer of the skin.

The dermis is the living skin layer.

Blood flows through capillaries in the dermis.

Underneath the epidermis there is a living layer called the **dermis**. This is where the blood goes when it reaches the skin, and where there are **nerves** that help you sense and feel. Blood keeps the living layer alive by giving the skin cells oxygen and food.

Blood helps you to cool down when you are hot. When you run about and get hot, your face may go red. This is because your blood vessels have got wider and wider to help get rid of the heat in your body.

It also helps you warm up. When you are cold, the blood vessels get narrower, and this helps to keep heat in your body.

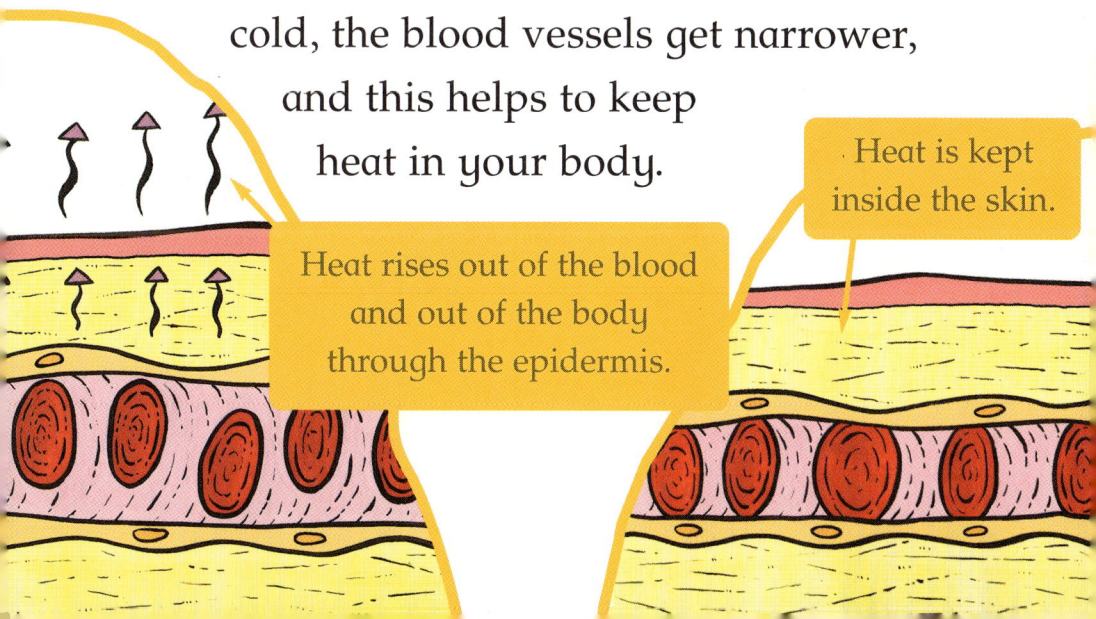

Heat rises out of the blood and out of the body through the epidermis.

Heat is kept inside the skin.

What does blood do in the muscles?

Your muscles give you your shape. You would look like a skeleton without them! Every time you move a finger, or make a face, you are using muscles. You cannot move without them. And every time your muscles work they need a good blood supply.

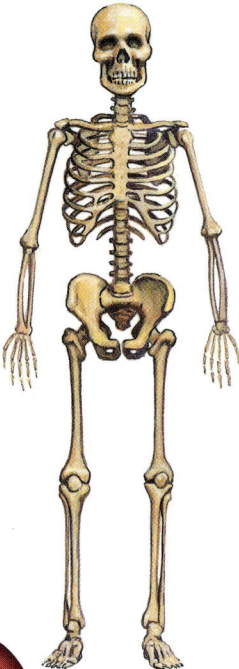

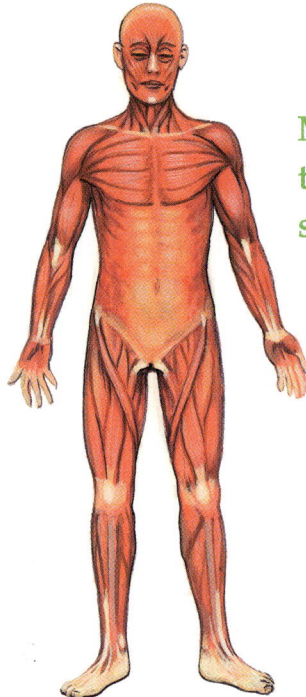

Muscles give the human skeleton shape.

When you run, your muscles have to work very hard indeed.

The cells in the muscles must get energy immediately! Your brain tells your blood to rush to the muscles being used, to give them extra oxygen and glucose for energy. And you can keep running as long as your blood has enough glucose to supply the muscles in your legs!

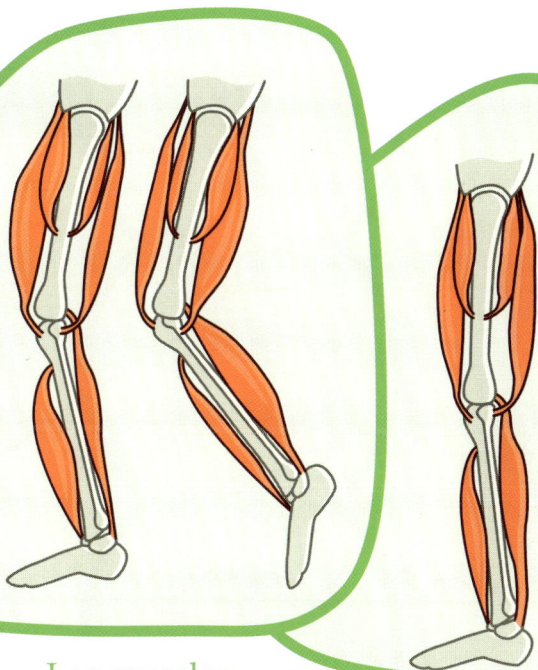

Leg muscles, active and resting.

FACTS

- You have 600 muscles in your body.

- Resting muscles need only 20 per cent of the body's blood supply, but active muscles can use up 80 per cent!

23

Why does a cut stop bleeding?

If you fall and graze your knees, or cut yourself on something sharp, blood flows out of your broken skin. Then, after a while, it stops!

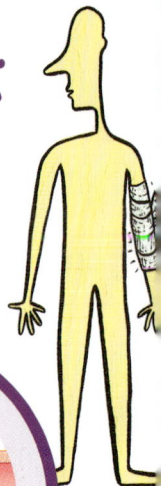

FACT

- Platelets are the smallest blood cells. They are actually made of broken bits of other blood cells. Usually you have between 300,000 and 500,000 platelets in every cubic millimetre of blood.

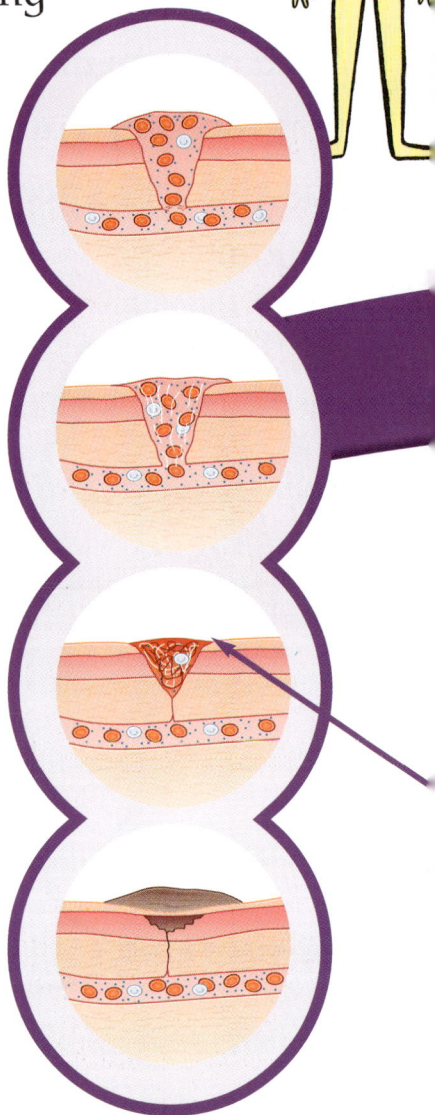

Your blood platelets have raced into action. They are the body's own sticking plaster – quickly plugging up the hole with a sticky clot.

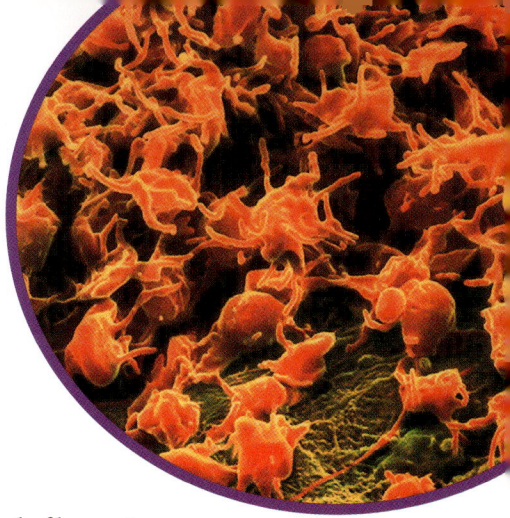

Once the blood has stopped flowing, the platelets make a network of stringy threads.

These make the clot stronger and harder, like a dam!

Your grazed knee now has a scab to protect the damaged skin while it heals itself. It will fall off when a new thin layer of skin has formed underneath. But be careful, because that new skin is very soft and can easily get hurt again.

When the skin is broken, blood flows out. Platelets and fibrin form threads over the wound to form a scab.

What happens when a baby is growing?

When a baby is growing inside its mother, it cannot feed itself. So for nearly forty weeks it gets food from its mother's blood.

A mother's body makes 30 per cent more blood to feed her growing baby. The baby cannot breathe like we do, so it also gets the oxygen it needs from its mother's blood. It flows from the mother to a spongy bump on her womb called the **placenta**.

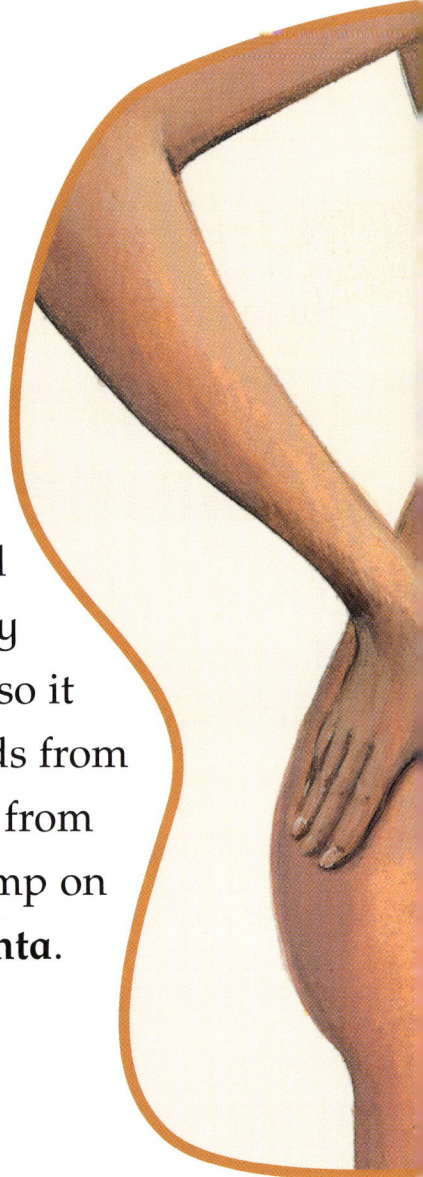

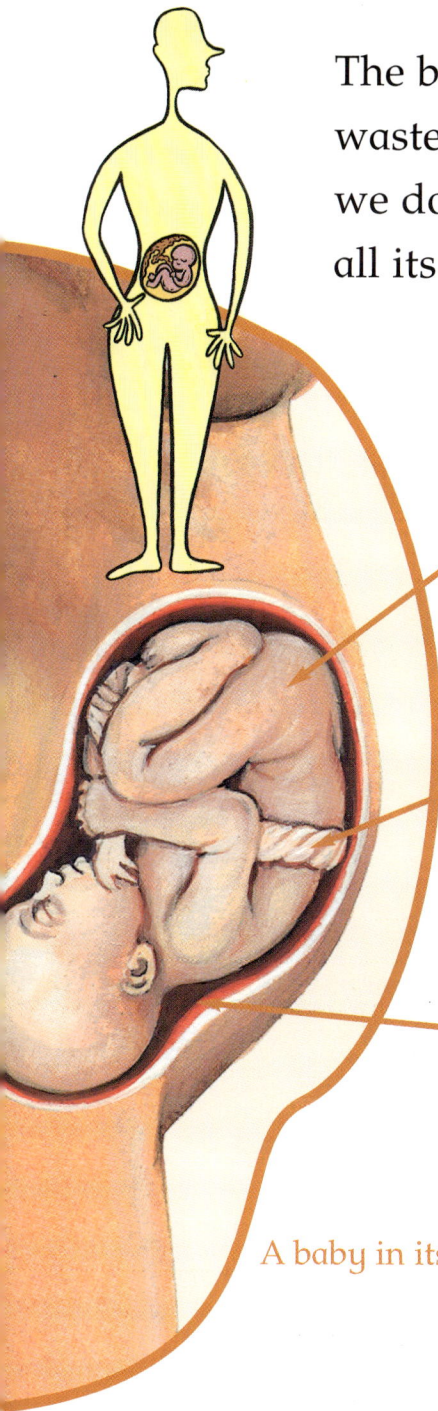

The baby cannot get rid of the waste products and poisons like we do either, so it gives its mother all its waste too.

The baby grows in the mother's **womb**.

The **umbilical cord** carries the baby's blood supply to the placenta.

The **placenta** is where the mother's and baby's blood vessels meet.

A baby in its mother's womb.

27

What happens when we get ill?

You can't see germs, but they are all around, on our food, our skin, and in the air. Sometimes they get into our bodies. If your blood is healthy it will fight the germs.

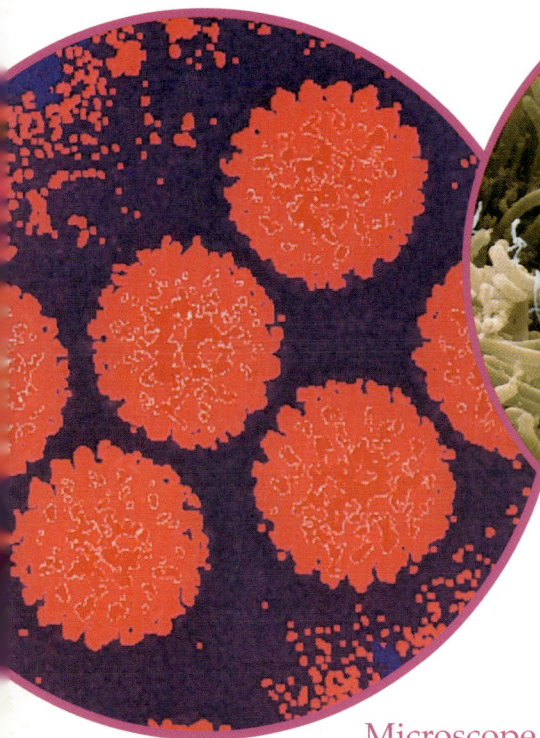

Microscope photo of common virus.

Microscope photo of common bacterium.

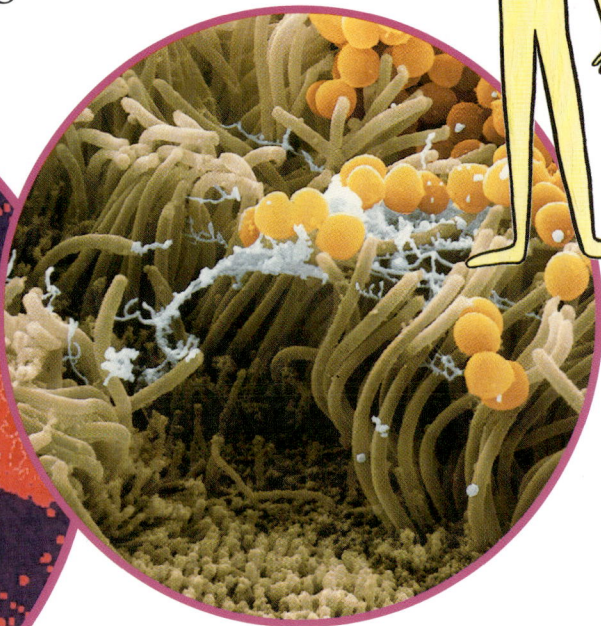

There are armies of white blood cells in your body, ready to fight bacteria and viruses when they invade. When you sneeze, you know they have invaded. The large white blood cells hunt the germs down, and swallow them, or send out deadly chemicals to kill them. When you are feeling very ill (and you have lots of germs), your body may have to make more white blood cells than usual in order to get rid of them all.

A white blood cell gobbling up a germ.

- White blood cells and plasma together make **lymph**. This fluid travels in special vessels round the body, and helps fight germs in every cell.

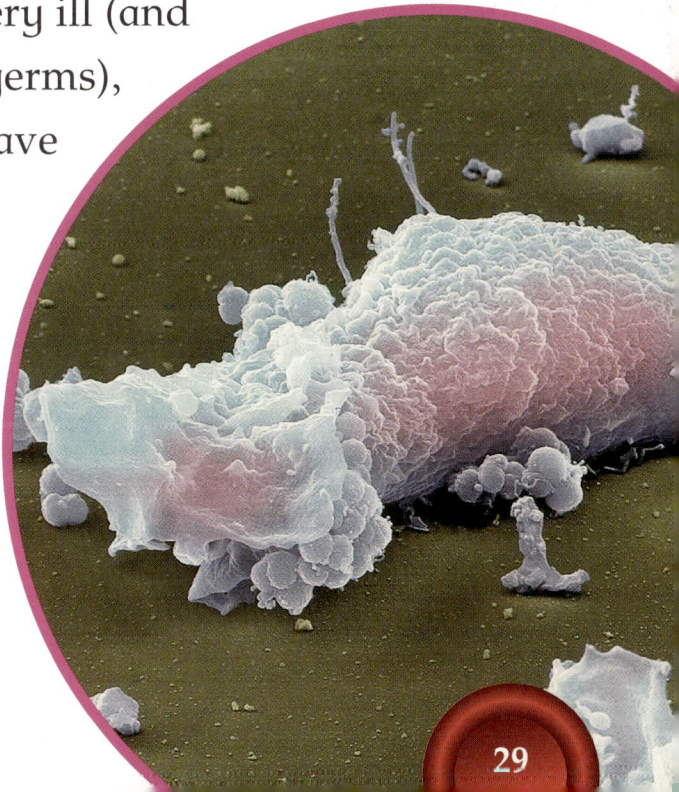

Blood's journey round the body

This is a summary of where your blood goes and what happens to it in each part of the body.

The heart

The heart is the body's pump. It sends blood through vessels all round the body.

The lungs

When your blood reaches the lungs it gets oxygen from the air to take to the cells all over the body.

The small intestine

The small intestine is where digesting food becomes small enough to pass through the intestine walls into surrounding blood vessels.

The brain

The brain needs blood to feed it oxygen and food, and to take away its waste gases.

The liver

The liver decides whether your body needs to store the energy from your food or use it straight away. It also gets rid of the poisons from your blood.

The kidneys

The kidneys filter out waste from water in the body's blood. They keep the body's salt and water levels just right.

The muscles

The muscles need the oxygen and glucose in your blood to allow you to move.

The skin

Blood keeps the living layer of the skin alive by giving it food and oxygen. Blood also helps you cool down or warm up.

Glossary

carbon dioxide the waste gas from cells that is breathed out from the lungs

carotid artery one of two arteries in the neck that take blood to the face and brain

consciousness the state of knowing what is happening (being aware)

energy power the body gains when oxygen gets to work on the food we eat

glucose a sugar that the body must have to make energy

molecules very small particles which make up all substances

nerves thread like fibres that help the body sense things

oxygen one of the gases in air, which we must breathe in to stay alive

protein one of the three main kinds of food, needed by all living things

valves flaps inside veins that let blood flow one way only (back to the heart)